D is for Desert

A World Deserts Alphabet

Written by Barbara Gowan
Illustrated by Gijsbert van Frankenhuyzen

Aa

Around one-third of the land surface of Planet Earth is desert. Deserts may be covered in dust, stones, or snow. They may be oceans of sand or rivers of ice, mountain peaks, sand dunes, or rocky plains. All deserts share one characteristic: there is little water available. A desert receives less than 10 inches (25 centimeters) of rain a year, and most of it comes in the form of violent storms. Because desert air is so dry and the sun's rays are so strong, any water evaporates quickly. Deserts like the Sahara in northern Africa and the Thar in India and Pakistan have daytime temperatures so high that an egg can fry on the sand.

Not all deserts are hot. Cold deserts like the Gobi in China and Mongolia and the Patagonian Desert in Argentina are more frigid than a freezer. Fog and snow bring moisture to cold deserts. The land near the North and South Poles is a desert because nearly all the water is locked up in sheets of ice.

The cold Atacama in South America is the most arid desert in the world. Rain rarely falls, but fog rolls in from the sea. Coastal residents harvest the fog by catching the mist on nets. The moisture drips into a trough and then is piped into the village, providing water for these desert dwellers.

Arid begins with the letter A.
It's a word that means very dry.
For 400 years in the Atacama Desert,
no rain fell from the sky.

The Bactrian camel can live without food for months at a time. The camel stores fat in its two humps. This fat can be converted to energy when food is scarce. The humps lean and droop on a hungry camel. When thirsty, the camel soaks up water like a sponge, drinking 30 gallons (114 liters) in only 13 minutes.

This animal is well adapted for life in the harsh, rocky, and cold deserts of Mongolia and China. Its shaggy winter coat of thick hair and underwool insulates it against the frigid nights, when temperatures can drop to -29° Fahrenheit (-34° Celsius). Large chunks of fur are quickly shed in the summer as the desert heat soars to over 100°F (38°C). Long, silky eyelashes, see-through third eyelids, bushy eyebrows, ears lined with fur, and nostrils that can be pinched shut protect the camel during a sandstorm. This well-designed pack animal is capable of carrying heavy loads. Wide, flat footpads help it traverse the rocky terrain.

There are many domestic camels, but the wild Bactrian camel is an endangered species with fewer than 1,000 individuals alive today.

B is for the Bactrian camel.
It has two humps to store rich fat
that provides energy when plants are scarce
in its rocky desert habitat.

Bb

The word *cactus* comes from the Greek word *kaktos*, which means "spiny plant." Cactus spines can be stiff, papery, wooly, curved, or needlelike. From being so small that they are almost invisible to being as long as a pencil, cactus spines are colored white, yellow, brown, black, or red. Bands of colored spines line up around the stem of the rainbow hedgehog cactus.

If a cactus had leaves, it would lose too much moisture in the drying desert winds. Spines are modified leaves and a way to conserve water. Hairy spines provide shade from the intense rays of the sun. At night they trap dew, which dribbles down to the roots. Spiky spines discourage most hungry animals. The jumping cholla (CHOY-ah) relies on its barb-tipped spines to stick to passing animals. The hitchhiking cactus eventually gets knocked off, takes root, and grows a new plant.

A cactus is called a succulent. It stores water in its pads and stem. The pleated shape of the barrel cactus allows it to expand when it rains and store water like a sponge. Its waxy skin seals in moisture. The hot Chihuahuan Desert in north central Mexico and southwestern United States is home to 350 species, one-fifth of all the world's known cacti.

Cactus begins with the letter C.
This desert plant with a waxy skin
is protected by spines
as sharp as a pin.

D is for Death Valley,
   a place of scorching heat.
Here the sun bakes the land
   as dry and hard as concrete.

Dd

Welcome to Furnace Creek in Death Valley National Park, the hottest and driest place in North America. Here, air temperatures reach over 100° Fahrenheit (38° Celsius) for four consecutive months. The desert floor can be even 40 degrees hotter. Annual rainfall averages less than 2 inches (5 centimeters) in this Mojave Desert park, and there have been some years with no recorded rain.

Death Valley lies in a long, narrow basin walled in by steep mountain ranges. The sun heats the desert soil and rocks, and the hot air becomes trapped in the valley.

Badwater Basin, the lowest place in North America, lies 282 feet (86 meters) below sea level. Shallow pools filled with minerals dissolved from rocks form here after flash floods. Because of the arid climate, water evaporates quickly, leaving a salt flat coated with a crust of sparkling white salt crystals.

Park visitors can explore dry waterfalls in marble canyons, snow-capped mountain peaks, sand dunes, volcanic craters, and the Devil's Golf Course, where jagged spires of rock salt cover the ground.

E e

E is for Erg,
a sea of sand grains
stretching for hundreds of miles
on a flat, wind-swept terrain.

An erg looks like a sea of sand. It may have dunes as tall as skyscrapers or vast plains of sand (called sand sheets).

Sandstorms driven by fierce winds shape an erg. When a shrub or boulder gets in the path of the windblown sand, a dune can form. Over time, sand piles up into a huge mound. If the wind gusts from only one direction, a barchan (a dune shaped like a crescent moon) forms. A star dune results from wind blowing from many directions. A long ridge with a swordlike crest is a *seif* dune and can extend for over 120 miles (193 kilometers). Large ergs, or sand seas, have taken shape over one million years and can be easily seen from satellites in space.

The largest erg in the world is located on the Arabian Peninsula. Rub`al-Khali (the empty quarter) is the size of Texas and extends into four countries—Saudi Arabia, Oman, Yemen, and the United Arab Emirates. Beneath this vast sea of sand lie enormous quantities of the world's major energy source, oil.

Dark storm clouds build up in the sky. Lightning flashes and thunder cracks. Huge raindrops develop into a torrential downpour. The summer monsoon has arrived in the desert southwest of the United States. The rain falls so hard and so fast that the parched earth cannot soak up all the water. The run-off flows like a raging river into a channel called a dry wash, or arroyo.

The flash flood brings needed water to desert plants. Surface roots suck up rain quickly. The shallow roots of the saguaro cactus extend in every direction around the plant and act like sponges, bringing water to the stem, where it is stored. The pleats on the cactus's trunk expand as it swells with as much as 5 tons (4.5 metric tons) of water.

The summer thunderstorm wakes up the buried Couch's spadefoot. This amphibian searches for a puddle where it absorbs water through its belly skin and then mates. Eggs hatch within a day, and tadpoles change into adults in less than two weeks. Using their "spades," the black, hard-edged scrapers on their hind feet, they dig into the soil and wait for next year's rain storm.

F f

F is for Flash Flood.
When torrential rain comes pouring down,
it's too much water for
the dry, hard ground.

G is for the Gobi Desert
where dinosaur skeletons are found.
This rocky region in central Asia
attracts the fossil hound.

The Gobi is like a treasure chest holding the world's richest and most diverse deposits of dinosaur and early mammal bones from more than 80 million years ago. Expeditions of paleontologists have been unearthing fossils from the pebble-strewn desert since 1923, when a dinosaur nest with eggs was discovered. During the first three hours of a 1993 expedition, scientists excavated fossils of 60 dinosaurs, mammals, and lizards—that's one find every three minutes! Skeletons from the armored, club-tailed Ankylosaurus, the parrot-lizard Psittacosaurus, and the meat-eating Velociraptor were identified.

The cold Gobi Desert spreads across southern Mongolia and northern China. The Himalaya Mountains block rain-carrying clouds from reaching the inland plateau. Temperatures are extreme, ranging from a frigid winter night of -45° Fahrenheit (-43° Celsius) to a scorching summer day over 100°F (38°C). This remote, stony, and nearly waterless place lures the adventurous fossil hunter to its rocky outcrops in search of clues to life from long ago.

Haboob begins with the letter H.
Whirling wind and swirling sand,
this massive wall of dust
completely covers the land.

It's daytime, but the sky is black. A moving mountain of dust blocks the sun. Gusts of wind dump grit and debris that wipe out roads and close down airports. This intense sandstorm is called a haboob, from the Arabic word *habb*, meaning "wind." It forms when a thunderstorm collapses and a powerful downdraft blasts outward, picking up loose sand. Arizona and Texas experience haboobs during the summer monsoon season. The Sahara city of Khartoum in the Sudan averages 24 haboobs a year.

Desert dust drifts around the world, affecting the environment in different ways. Satellite images show dust floating 15,000 feet (4.6 kilometers) above the earth's surface. Dried sediment weighing 2.2 billion tons (2 billion metric tons) travels through the atmosphere each year. Sand from the Sahara Desert replenishes mineral nutrients in the Amazon Rainforest but pollutes Caribbean coral reefs. Dust clouds can block the sunlight from warming the ocean's surface, resulting in cooler waters. Particles from China's Taklimakan Desert were found in snow in the French Alps. They blew across the Pacific Ocean, North America, and the Atlantic Ocean—more than 12,000 miles (19,300 kilometers)—in just two weeks.

H
h

Unusual survival strategies are necessary to live in the harsh desert. Along the southwest coast of Africa lies the Namib Desert, home to invertebrates with unique methods of obtaining water. The darkling beetle climbs to the top of a sand dune, faces the sea, and stands on its head with its long legs out-stretched. Fog condenses on its body and moisture trickles into its mouth. Another type of dune beetle digs trenches in the sand to trap the fog. The dancing white lady spider cartwheels down a dune to flee an enemy, and then hides in its burrow covered by a web camouflaged with sand.

Tarantulas and scorpions live in deserts such as the Sahara and Gobi as well as those in the southwestern United States. They escape the daytime heat in cool burrows. These noc-turnal predators are sensitive to vibrations and use venom to paralyze their prey—insects, spiders, and small lizards. The tarantula, a hand-sized, hairy spider, kills with a deadly bite. Its fangs secrete juices that liquefy the victim's body. Through strawlike openings, the spider sucks up its meal. The scorpion lies in wait, grabs its prey with its large pin-cers, and injects venom from the stinger on its arched tail.

I is for Invertebrates.
These animals without a backbone
like insects, spiders, and scorpions,
have adapted to their desert home.

Jj

The Joshua tree is not really a tree. This weird-looking, tall cousin of the lily is a yucca (YUCK-uh). It can live for over 900 years and grow to 40 feet (12 meters) in height. Thick branches covered in stiff, daggerlike leaves grow like twisted arms. After the spring rains, flower clusters appear on long stalks at the end of each branch. They open at night and emit a musty smell that attracts a type of tiny moth.

Joshua trees depend on this moth for pollination because their flowers' pollen is too heavy to be carried by the wind. The yucca moth collects the pollen, patting it into a ball. It visits another blossom, stuffs the pollen ball into the new flower, and then lays eggs on it. The pollen ball fertilizes the Joshua tree, so it can produce seeds. When the seeds mature, they will provide food for the moth larvae, or caterpillars. Both the plant and the moth benefit from this partnership.

Joshua Tree National Park in California protects these unique and important plants of the Mojave Desert.

J is for the Joshua tree,
with flower clusters of greenish white.
They sit atop its armlike branches
and create an unusual sight.

K k

A kangaroo rat can leap 9 feet (3 meters) in one hop to escape predators! Aided by its large rear legs and long, tufted tail, which it uses for balance, this rodent is an expert jumper.

The kangaroo rat is well adapted for desert life. It does not drink water, and it does not sweat or pant. Its digestive system converts its food—starchy seeds—into energy and water. Its highly efficient kidneys produce little waste.

This nocturnal critter escapes the midday heat in its underground burrow. Kangaroo rats are construction engineers and build an intricate tunnel system of sleeping, living, and storage chambers. The pantry may hold several bushels of seeds. These diggers are constantly remodeling their homes.

The kangaroo rat communicates by drumming its feet, chattering its teeth, and by squealing and grunting.

Found in North American deserts, the kangaroo rat could be a cousin to the gerbil of Africa and the jerboa of Asia; they look alike and have similar adaptations to desert life.

Kangaroo rat begins with K.
What a jumping superstar!
A tufted tail and oversized legs
allow it to leap quite far.

Thorny devil, Gila (HEE-lah) monster, Australian bearded dragon! The desert is home to a variety of lizards, many with fierce-sounding names. These cold-blooded reptiles manage their body temperature by scurrying in and out of the shade.

Lizards have unusual ways of defending themselves. Have you ever seen a lizard doing push-ups? That's its way of getting the attention of other lizards that have entered its territory. Bright pink, black, and orange beaded scales on the 2-foot-long (61-centi-meter-long) Gila monster serve as a warning to alert predators that it is poisonous. The western banded gecko squeaks noisily when bothered. The spines of the horned lizard make it an unpopular meal. It can make its body swell, jump forward with a hiss, and even shoot blood from its eyes as a way to frighten predators. The chuckwalla, a large lizard with a big belly, defends itself by crawl-ing into a narrow rock crevice and inflating itself so that it cannot be pulled out by a predator. The fringe-toed lizard swiftly van-ishes by diving into the loose sand and "swimming" beneath the surface by wig-gling its body. All these lizards live in the Sonoran Desert.

L is for a Lizard
basking in the desert sun.
Until its body gets too hot—
then to the shade it runs.

L1

M is for Mineral deposits
  discovered under rock and sand.
Copper, silver, oil, and gold
  make the desert valuable land.

Deserts possess a wealth of minerals. Geologists estimate 1.5 billion carats of diamonds and other gemstones, such as amethyst and topaz, lie beneath the coastal sands of the Namib Desert in southwest Africa.

Ores are rocks that contain metals like gold, silver, copper, and iron. The Atacama Desert in South America is the site of the largest copper mines in the world. The richest deposits of iron ore (used in the production of steel) and uranium (the raw material for nuclear fuels) are located in the Australian deserts. In the Great Basin Desert, water evaporates from seasonal pools, leaving behind mineral crystals such as salt, gypsum, and borax. Gypsum is used to make plaster, drywall, and blackboard chalk; borax is an important detergent. An ocean of oil lies beneath the sands of the Arabian Peninsula, bringing riches to countries in the Middle East.

Management of desert resources is a difficult job. Environmentalists are concerned because mineral exploration and mining disturbs the desert ecosystem. Money from the sale of mineral rights is often not fairly distributed to native desert people.

M
m

Nocturnal begins with the letter N.
It means active at night.
These animals will hunt for food
in the cool desert moonlight.

The desert is awake at night! Summertime temperatures in the Sonoran Desert may drop from 120° Fahrenheit (49° Celsius) at mid-day to 70°F (21°C) at night. This temperature shift creates dew from the small amount of moisture in the air. Nocturnal animals search for food and avoid predators in the cool, moist darkness.

Nighttime predators usually have large eyes and sensitive ears. The round, yellow eyes of the great horned owl face forward and provide binocular vision and precise depth perception. This stealth hunter flies on silent wings. The oversized ears of the kit fox magnify the sounds of its favorite food, the kangaroo rat. Most bats navigate by echolocation. The bat emits a high-pitched sound that bounces off objects and echoes back to them. Rattlesnakes, scorpions, and most rodents are nocturnal. The jackrabbit, javelina, bobcat, and coyote are nocturnal and also crepuscular (active at dawn and dusk).

Some cacti bloom at night. Each flower blossom has only one night to attract a pollinator. The strong, sweet smell of the queen of the night flower attracts the sphinx moth. Nectar-feeding bats visit the large creamy white saguaro cactus flowers.

O o

Did you know that Las Vegas, Nevada, is built on the site of an oasis? In 1829 a Mexican trader searching for water in the Mojave Desert discovered a spring in a water-rich valley. He named it *Las Vegas,* which means "the meadows" in Spanish. It became an important rest stop where pioneer travelers could replenish their water supply. Today it is a vibrant city in the desert.

Water gets trapped underground in layers of rock called aquifers. An oasis is formed when trapped water is forced through cracks in the rock to the earth's surface and forms a spring or pool. Lush vegetation, especially grasses and palm trees, grows near these water sources. Oasis towns were important marketplaces along the Silk Road, the major caravan trade route between China and the West, for more than 2,000 years.

Satellite images from space can locate hidden water pools under the desert floor. Modern drilling equipment can reach the water and create a new oasis.

O is for Oasis
where palm trees grow.
Springs bring water to the surface
from rock layers below.

Antarctica is a land of extremes. It is the coldest, iciest, windiest, highest, and driest continent on Earth. This polar desert is blanketed by a thick ice sheet containing 90 percent of all the ice on the planet. Blizzards with hurricane-force winds cause whiteout conditions. Inland mountains surround the McMurdo Dry Valleys, where winds blow away the snow, leaving a Martianlike landscape of bare rock. Rainfall rarely reaches this desert valley floor, and then only a few drops fall. The lowest temperature on Earth, -128.6° Fahrenheit (-89.2° Celsius), was recorded at a research station there.

Antarctica is called the "land of the long day." The sun never sets during summer at the South Pole, resulting in six months of daylight. Because the white landscape reflects the intense rays of the sun, sunglasses are essential to protect the eyes from burning.

Seas around Antarctica are rich in marine life, ranging from microscopic plankton to the blue whale. The largest land animal is a wingless insect just .5 inch (13 millimeters) long. Nonflowering plants such as mosses and lichens grow on less than 1 percent of the continent. Algae live in the ice. No people live permanently on Antarctica.

P p

P is for Polar deserts,
a white land of ice and snow.
Here temperatures may plummet
to one hundred below zero.

More than 7,000 years ago, Persian farmers constructed underground tunnel systems called *qanats*. This water delivery system provided people living in arid mountain basins with water to grow crops. At the foot of the mountain, a deep well was dug to tap into the aquifer, or underground water supply. Skilled workers carefully excavated downward-sloping, narrow underground tunnels that transported water to the villages. This traditional water-harvesting technique is still used in western China, northern Africa, and on the Arabian Peninsula.

Surface canals have been used to irrigate farms in the desert southwest of North America for more than 3,000 years. The ancient Hohokam Indians engineered an extensive canal system that brought river water to their crops of corn, beans, squash, and cotton. Today's modern canals in Phoenix, Arizona, were built along this original network.

Qanat begins with the letter Q.
It's a tunnel built by humans
that transports cool, flowing water
to desert homes and gardens.

Mountains can create deserts! Picture the Sierra Nevada mountain range in California. The mountains force the warm, moist air from the Pacific Ocean to rise. The air cools as it rises, clouds form, and rain or snow falls on the peaks. The air mass crosses the range and sweeps down the other side, but it no longer carries much moisture. The hot Mojave and Sonoran deserts, and the cold Great Basin Desert lie in this dry rain shadow. The cold Patagonian Desert in southern Argentina lies in the rain shadow of the Andes Mountains.

The Gobi and Taklimakan deserts in central Asia are too far away from the sea to benefit from its moisture and clouds. The air masses are dry when they reach these cold inland deserts.

A desert can form next to an ocean. Cold water currents chill the air flowing inland, producing a thick fog blanket that traps moisture. Rain clouds cannot develop. South America's Atacama Desert and the Namib in Africa are coastal deserts.

Warm air rises near the equator, sheds rain, and then moves on toward the poles, blowing hot, dry wind across the area between the Tropic of Cancer and the Tropic of Capricorn. This belt of arid land is home to the hot Sahara and Arabian deserts.

R is for Rain shadow
　　where mountains block moist air.
Rain pours down on one side,
　　leaving the other side dry and bare.

The Sahara Desert is listed in the *Guinness World Records* for its size and its temperatures. It is the largest hot desert on Earth (almost the size of the United States) and crosses 11 countries in Africa. Heat waves shimmer above the desert floor, where the hottest temperature, 136° Fahrenheit (58° Celsius), was recorded—and that was in the shade! Nighttime temperatures can plummet to below zero in the mountains. Average annual rainfall is just 3 inches (8 centimeters).

Winds can churn up to 200 million tons (181 million metric tons) of sediment, making the Sahara Desert the biggest source of dust in the world. Whirlwinds called simooms carry masses of sand, changing the shape of the dunes along its path. Barren, waterless plains of gravel cover most of this desert.

Mountain peaks high enough to be capped with snow are a result of past volcanic explosions. Salt flats were formed when ancient lakes evaporated.

Siwa Oasis in Egypt has been a thriving trading center since the time of Alexander the Great (356–323 BCE). This lush, fertile oasis is fed by underground springs and is a green island in an ocean of sand. The Sahara Desert is one of our planet's natural wonders.

S is for Sahara,
     the largest hot desert in the land.
Stretching across North Africa
          are mountains, dunes, and seas of sand.

For thousands of years, the Tuareg (TWAH-reg) tribe has operated trade routes across the Sahara. These skilled riders would travel for months on one-humped camels called dromedaries to collect salt to sell at a market hundreds of miles away.

Tuareg men are recognizable by their indigo *tagelmust*, a 20-foot-long (6-meter-long) blue veil and turban. This cotton cloth is wrapped around the head, leaving only a slit for the eyes to protect them from blowing sand. Tuareg men believe the tagelmust also wards off evil spirits that try to enter through the mouth.

A typical meal for these traveling traders, or nomads, would be camel's milk with dried dates or *taguella*, a flat bread baked under the sand.

Life is changing for the Tuaregs. They once owned much of the Sahara, but today national boundaries make it difficult to cross borders to trade. Trucks can deliver goods faster than camel caravans can. Drought has devastated their herds. Many have been forced to give up their nomad life and settle as farmers or city dwellers.

T is for the Tuareg people,
masters of the salt trade.
Caravanning across the Sahara,
it looks like a camel parade!

T t

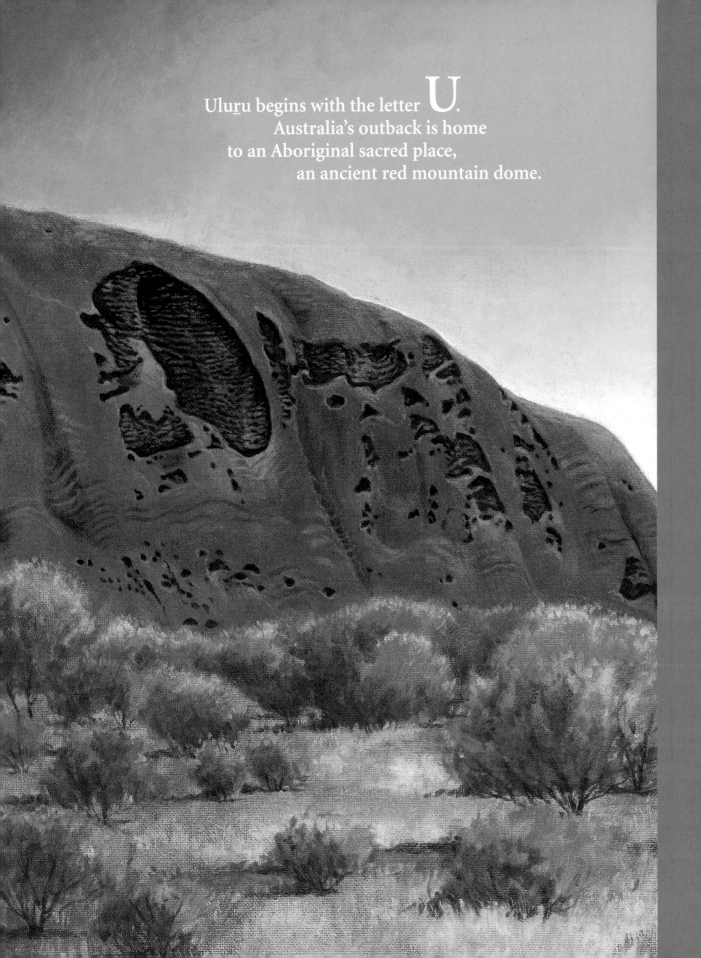

Uluṟu begins with the letter U.
Australia's outback is home
to an Aboriginal sacred place,
an ancient red mountain dome.

In the heart of the flat Australian desert outback looms a blood-red mountain. Previously known as Ayers Rock, it has been given back its original Aboriginal name, *Uluṟu*. The native Aṉangu people believe they have a spiritual connection with nature. Uluṟu is sacred to the Aṉangu and has been designated a UNESCO World Heritage site for its geological and cultural importance.

This island mountain (also called an inselberg) remained after the original mountain range was worn away by the elements. The massive sandstone dome is over 1,100 feet (335 meters) high and nearly 6 miles (10 kilometers) around. It appears to change color as light strikes it during the day. Uluṟu glows red at sunset.

Hot deserts rule Australia, covering nearly two-thirds of the continent. Rust-red dunes extend in rows for hundreds of miles in the Great Sandy Desert. The first explorers to the Sturt Stony Desert were faced with sharp rocks that cut their boots and shredded their horses' hooves. Large flightless emus hunt for grain and insects while western gray kangaroos bound through the rugged desert outback in search of grasses to graze on.

U u

Viper begins with the letter V.
This snake with poison glands
strikes out at its next victim
while hiding in the sand.

The Sahara sand viper is an ambush hunter. Using rapid sideways movements, the snake burrows into the loose sand. Only its eyes and upper lip are visible. The forked tongue flicks in and out, retrieving sensory information. It waits for a passing lizard, rodent, or small mammal, and once the prey is detected, the snake strikes. Its long, sharp fangs inject a deadly dose of venom from the poison glands above the hollow front teeth. The venom attacks the blood cells, causing the prey to die quickly. A large meal can satisfy the snake's food and water requirements for several weeks. When the sand viper is not hunting, it rests in the coolness of its underground lair.

Rattlesnakes are members of the pit viper family. These snakes have a small pit between each eye and nostril. The pits are sensitive to the body heat of the snake's prey. Rings of dry skin on the tip of the tail form a rattle. When the snake is disturbed, it sends out a warning by vigorously shaking its tail. A rattlesnake can travel quickly by coiling its body and moving diagonally across the hot sand.

W is for Wind and Water.
These are Mother Nature's tools
that carve the landscape to create
canyons, mesas, and hoodoos.

Wind and water are the powerful forces in nature that continually shape the desert landscape. Violent windstorms can last for days, picking up sand from one place and depositing it thousands of miles away.

On the Colorado Plateau in Utah's Canyonlands National Park, wind-blasted gritty sand chisels away at the bases of rock columns, creating mushroom-shaped formations. A mesa is a mountain with a flat top and steep sides; its shape was formed after erosion wore away the softer rock landscape. And totem polelike pillars called hoodoos are shaped by the erosion of rocks of varying hardness.

Flash floods carrying sand and stone scour the desert floor. The cutting power of the Colorado River in northern Arizona is evident in the layers of rock it carved through to create the 1-mile-deep (1.6-kilometer-deep) Grand Canyon. In Bryce Canyon National Park in the Great Basin Desert, winter snow melts and water trickles into the joints, or cracks, between the rocks. It freezes and forms an ice wedge, widening the crack until the rock breaks off.

The desert is home to awesome landforms sculpted by wind and water.

A xerophyte (ZEER-eh-fite) is a water-thrifty plant. A cactus, for example, has a network of shallow roots to capture rain from even a light shower. This succulent then stores the rainwater in its swollen stems. A waxy coating and the lack of leaves are adaptations to minimize water loss.

The tiny leaves of desert trees and shrubs fold or even drop from the plant during times of drought. The ocotillo (o-keh-TEE-yo) shows evidence of recent rain when its thorny, pole-like branches become covered in green, and the tips bloom with clusters of red flowers. The paloverde (pah-lo-VER-dee) tree, meaning "green stick" in Spanish, has smooth, green bark and branches where photosynthesis (food making) occurs. Its deep root system allows it to tap into the groundwater. The creosote bush can go without rain for two years. The waxy leaf coating prevents water loss.

Many homes in desert cities like Phoenix and Las Vegas have xeriscapes (ZEER-uh-scapes), or landscapes that use water-conserving methods. To conserve water in xeriscapes, colored rocks are often used to replace grass.

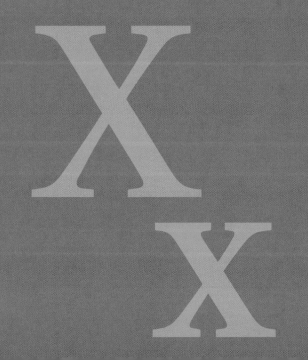

X
x

X is for Xerophyte,
a plant that grows where it's dry.
Well adapted to the desert
and its limited water supply.

A Mongolian herder and his family may move 50 times in a year! These nomads of central Asia travel in search of water and pasture for their sheep and goats. Their portable house is called a yurt (or ger) and is made of thick wool mats attached to a foldaway wooden frame. It can be dismantled in less than an hour. The Bactrian camel serves as the moving van, carrying the family belongings, house and all, on its back.

The Bedouin nomads of the Arabian and Sahara deserts stay cool in tents made from loosely woven sheep, goat, or camel hair. Adjustable flaps allow cool breezes to circulate inside. Curtains divide the tent into rooms, and the family sits and sleeps on carpets.

In the Kalahari Desert of southern Africa, the San people (also called Bushmen), lead the primitive life of hunter-gatherers. In their campsite, haystack huts made of woven grass covering twig frames offer protection from summer rainstorms. They are similar to wickiups, dwellings of nomadic Native Americans, like the Apaches, of the Southwest deserts.

Yurt begins with the letter Y,
a wool tent, round and white.
It keeps a nomad family warm
on a cold Gobi Desert night.

Z

Z is for Zion National Park,
a refuge for bighorn sheep.
Here rams and ewes can be seen
on slopes that are rocky and steep.

CRACK—loud as a rifle shot, the sound echoes through the canyons as desert bighorn sheep compete in a head-banging contest. The battle begins when two male sheep, or rams, snort loudly and size each other up by tilting their heads to display their massive curled horns. They rear up on their hind legs and then charge at speeds of up to 20 miles (32 kilometers) per hour and butt their heads. The clash may last as long as 24 hours and ends when one ram backs down. This fight for dominance determines who gets to mate with the ewes, or female sheep, in the herd.

The steep, rocky slopes of Zion National Park in the Mojave Desert in southwestern Utah are an ideal habitat for the desert bighorn sheep. Long ago, there were many sheep here, but disease and hunting by early settlers killed them all. Today's herd of approximately 160 desert bighorn sheep are descendants of 12 sheep that were released in the park in the 1970s. The Adopt-a-Bighorn program in Zion National Park (see www.zionpark.org for more information) encourages visitors to help protect this unique desert animal.

What is a Desert?

A desert is a bone-dry place. Most of the world's deserts are hot deserts with scorching daytime temperatures for most of the year. The Sahara Desert in Africa and the Mojave Desert in North America are hot deserts. Cold deserts have daytime temperatures that can dip below freezing for part of the year. Many cold deserts receive half their moisture in the form of snow. The Gobi Desert in central Asia and the Great Basin Desert in North America are cold deserts. The polar desert of Antarctica is frigid.

There are many deserts above the equator along the Tropic of Cancer (23° N latitude) and below the equator along the Tropic of Capricorn (23° S latitude). Near the equator, the climate is warm and wet. As air moves farther away from the equator, it gets sucked down and becomes a dry wind. The wind is very strong over the Tropic of Cancer and the Tropic of Capricorn. Rain clouds are rare. The deserts in Africa and Australia lie in these areas.

Some deserts, like the Taklimakan and Gobi in central Asia, are dry because they are located in the middle of the continent, far from an ocean. By the time the air reaches the center of the continent, it has dropped all its moisture and is very dry.

Mountains can act like a wind barrier or rain shadow. Moist clouds dump all their rain or snow on one side of a mountain range, creating a dry desert on the other side. The North American deserts are rain shadow deserts.

For more information on and images of deserts around the world, please check out the websites listed below.

www.geology.com/records/sahara-desert-map.shtml
http://mbgnet.mobot.org/sets/desert/index.htm

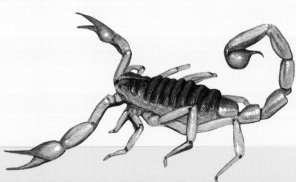

Glossary

aquifer: an underground layer of rock with tiny holes where water is trapped (see letter O)

arid: excessively dry or lacking moisture (see letter A)

arroyo (ah-ROY-oh): a Spanish word for a steep-sided gully or dry river bed carved by heavy rains (see letter F)

barchan (bahr-KAHN): a type of sand dune shaped like a crescent moon (see letter E)

cold-blooded: a body temperature that is controlled by the surrounding air or water (see letter L)

crepuscular: active in the cool morning and late afternoon (see letter N)

drought: an extended period without rain that can last for months or even years (see letter X)

echolocation: a way to find objects by listening to sounds bouncing off the object (see letter N)

ecosystem: the climate, water supply, and all living plants and animals in an area (see letter M)

erg: a huge sand sea that is covered by shifting sand hills called dunes (see letter E)

erosion: the slow, continual wearing away of rocks on the earth's surface by forces of wind and water (see letter W)

evaporate: to dissipate or convert into vapor, as in changing from a liquid to a gas (see letter A)

fog: a cloud, a mass of tiny water droplets, floating very close to the ground (see letter A)

haboob: a wall of dust that may form during a monsoon thunderstorm (see letter H)

hoodoo: an unusually shaped stone column formed by the wearing away of weaker rock layers (see letter W)

inselberg (IN-suhl-burg): a rocky hill formed by erosion and weathering that stands alone on a flat plain (see letter U)

insulate: to provide protection with a material that helps reduce the loss of heat (see letter B)

mesa (MAY-sah): a mountain with a flat top and steep sides (see letter W)

monsoon: a cool, moist wind that moves over hot, dry land, resulting in an extreme thunderstorm (see letter F)

nocturnal: active at night (see letter N)

oasis: a place in the desert with a constant source of water, usually from an underground spring (see letter O)

outcrops: huge pieces of solid rock that stick out above the soil (see letter G)

photosynthesis: the process by which green plants use sunlight to turn carbon dioxide and water into food (see letter X)

pollination: the transfer of pollen grains from one flower to another so a seed can form (see letter J)

qanat (kha-NAHT): a human-made water tunnel dug deep underground (see letter Q)

rain shadow: an area of dry land on the sheltered (downward) side of a mountain (see letter R)

secrete: to release a fluid, usually from the body (see letter I)

sediment: small particles of sand, dust, or grit (see letter H)

simoom: a hot, dry tornadolike wind that blows around masses of sand (see letter S)

succulent: a type of plant that stores water in its juicy stem, pads, or leaves (see letter A)

terrain: ground (see letter B)

torrential: heavy downpour (see letter F)

xerophyte (ZEER-eh-fite): a plant that is adapted to living in a dry habitat and needs little water to survive (see letter X)

To my botany professor at Notre Dame, Father McGrath, CSC,
who introduced me to the wonders of the desert plant world.

BARBARA

✷

To Pim & Friso

GIJSBERT

✷

ILLUSTRATOR'S ACKNOWLEDGMENTS

Andy McIntyre, John Ball Zoological Garden, Grand Rapids, MI
Megan Shannon, Preuss Pets, Lansing, MI
Tom and Nancy Dorey
R. D. Bartlett
Barbara Gowan
Felicia Macheske

Thanks to all these people for their help.

—GIJSBERT

Text Copyright © 2012 Barbara Gowan
Illustration Copyright © 2012 Gijsbert van Frankenhuyzen

Sleeping Bear Press®
315 E. Eisenhower Parkway, Suite 200
Ann Arbor, MI 48108
www.sleepingbearpress.com

Sleeping Bear Press is an imprint of Gale, a part of Cengage Learning.

10 9 8 7 6 5 4 3 2 1

Library of Congress Cataloging-in-Publication Data

Gowan, Barbara.
D is for desert : a world deserts alphabet / Barbara Gowan.
p. cm.
ISBN 978-1-58536-501-2
1. Desert ecology—Juvenile literature. 2. Alphabet books—Juvenile literature. I.
Frankenhuyzen, Gijsbert van, ill. II. Title.
QH541.5.D4G69 2012
577.54—dc23   2012007396

Printed by China Translation & Printing Services Limited,
Guangdong Province, China. 1st printing. 05/2012